Joseph's Journey
Volume 7

Reminiscence of Recuperation

Joseph's Journey
Volume 7

Reminiscence of Recuperation

by

Joseph Fram

Everlasting Publishing
Vancouver, Washington
USA

Joseph's Journey
Volume 7

Reminiscence of Recuperation

by
Joseph Fram

Library of Congress Control Number
2010906248

ISBN: 0-9824844-8-8

ISBN-13: 978-0-9824844-8-7

First Edition
Everlasting Publishing
P.O. Box 965
Vancouver, WA 98666-0965

REMINISCENCE OF RECUPERATION

RANDOM THOUGHTS OF A MAN TRYING TO
MAKE IT TO THE NEXT DAY, FOLLOWING A
HEARTBREAKING DIVORCE, WHEN ALL THAT
HE HAS LEFT IS THE GRACE OF GOD.

Table of Contents

MY OTHER WORLD
by
Joseph Fram

I SLIP INTO MY OTHER WORLD
SOMETIMES LATE AT NIGHT
TO ESCAPE FROM THE ONE I'M IN
TO MAKE THE WRONGS SEEM RIGHT

IT IS A WORLD WHERE I CAN DREAM
AND PLACE ALL THINGS JUST SO
I BLESS THOSE THINGS I CHERISH
AND LET THE OTHERS GO

I CALL UP CHILDHOOD PLAYMATES
THAT I WOULD LIKE TO SEE AGAIN
I CHANGE SOME THINGS I DIDN'T LIKE
AND MAKE OTHERS JUST THE SAME

MY OTHER WORLD IS FULL OF PEACE
THERE IS NO STRIFE IN ME
I DO NOT LET IN ANGER
I KEEP MY SPIRIT FREE

IT IS MY PRIVATE TIME WITH GOD
I SHARE THE TROUBLES OF THE DAY
WHEN WE HAVE HAD OUR TALK
THEY SOMEHOW GO AWAY

SILHOUETTE
by
Joseph Fram

I SAW A SILHOUETTE OF LOVE
WHEN FIRST MY MANHOOD GREETED ME
AND I MISTOOK THAT SILHOUETTE
FOR A LOVE THAT COULD NOT BE

THROUGH MY LIFE THAT SILHOUETTE
TOOK ALL THE LOVE THAT I COULD GIVE
SHE COULD NOT LOVE IN RETURN
FOR SHADOWS CAST WILL NEVER LIVE

IN MY MIND I CAN RECALL
JUST HOW I MADE THAT SILHOUETTE
THEN IT DANCED AWAY FROM ME
AND THOUGH NOT REAL I CAN'T FORGET

THEN I FOUND THAT SHADOWS CAST
COME FROM ONE WHO SHIELDS THE LIGHT
AND IF YOU LOVE A SILHOUETTE
SHE WILL BE GONE IN DARK OF NIGHT

BEWARE OF SILHOUETTES YOU CREATE
THEY MAY EXIST ONLY IN YOUR MIND
YOU CANNOT MAKE IT COME TO LIFE
FOR ONLY DARKNESS YOU WILL FIND

HOUSE OF CARDS
by
Joseph Fram

I HAD BUILT MY HOUSE OF CARDS
OH, SO NEATLY IN MY MIND
AT THE TIME I DIDN'T KNOW
THAT HOUSE I BUILT I'D NEVER FIND

MY LITTLE HOUSE OF CARDS
WAS BUILT WITH LOVE, HOPE AND SUCH
IT WAS NOT THE WORLDLY THING
I EVER CARED FOR VERY MUCH

I HOPED FOR LOVE AND LOVE'S RETURN
THESE CARDS WERE DEALT FOR LIFE
WHEN I THOUGHT I'D FOUND THE ONE
I BADE HER BE MY WIFE

THEN I GUESS MY HOUSE OF CARDS
AND HERS WERE NOT THE SAME
SHE TOOK MY HAND BUT NOT MY LOVE
SAD TO SAY SHE ONLY TOOK MY NAME

SADDER YET I NOW RECALL
WHAT PUT MY HOUSE OF CARDS TO DEATH
THAT FRAGILE DREAMS BUILT IN MY MIND
CAN TUMBLE WITH ONE PUFF OF BREATH

CAN'T ERASE A LOVE
by
Joseph Fram

I HAD TRIED TO HATE YOU
WHEN ANOTHER TOOK YOUR HEART
THEN YOU TOLD ME IT WAS OVER
AND NOW THAT WE MUST PART

HOW COULD YOU BE SO CRUEL
DASH ALL MY HOPES INTO THE GROUND
AFTER ALL THOSE YEARS TOGETHER
A NEW ROMANCE IS WHAT YOU FOUND

I NEVER THOUGHT OF CHEATING
BUT IT WAS ALWAYS ON YOUR MIND
I KNOW THE HURTING PART OF LOVE
I NEVER KNEW YOU'D BE THIS UNKIND

MY HURT HAS TURNED TO ACHING
I NOW HAVE A NIGHT AND DAY
THE LONELY HOURS I SPENT CRYING
SOMEHOW HAVE GONE AWAY

FOREVER THINGS HAVE CHANGED NOW
SINCE I TURNED TO GOD ABOVE
HATE NO LONGER CREEPS INTO MY MIND
BECAUSE YOU JUST CAN'T ERASE A LOVE

OLD MEMORIES
by
Joseph Fram

IT WAS A TIME OF LOVE AND JOY
YOUR HEART WAS YOUNG AND STRONG
A TIME THE WORLD WAS YOURS
YOU LIVED EACH NEW LOVE SONG

THERE WAS THE BEAUTY OF YOUR YOUTH
TIME WAS MOSTLY WHAT YOU HAD
WHEN YOUR HEART WAS BROKEN
TIME HEALED A HEART THAT'S SAD

WHEN YOU GAVE UP ALL YOUR DREAMS
TO MAKE MEMORIES OF A LOVE SO TRUE
THEY WERE TO LAST FOREVER
THAT'S WHAT YOUR HEART TOLD YOU TO DO

BUT YOUR FOREVER WAS ALL YOUR OWN
THE MEMORIES BUILT WERE NEVER SHARED
THE TRUST AND DREAMS WERE NEVER TAKEN
YOU GAVE LOVE TO ONE WHO NEVER CARED

SHE HAS GONE AND LEFT YOU CRYING
WHY DID SHE WAIT SO LONG TO PART
MEMORIES LIKE THAT CAN KILL YOU
DON'T LET OLD MEMORIES RULE YOUR HEART

SISTER HELEN
by
Joseph Fram

HELEN DEAR HELEN,
YOUR SMILE NEVER ENDS
EVERYONE YOU MEET
BECOME INSTANT FRIENDS

YOUR VOICE IS SO GENTLE
YOUR MANNER SO KIND
ONE'S LIFE IS FAR BETTER
IF YOU THEY SHOULD FIND

AS MY BIG SISTER
I KNEW LOVE FROM THE START
FROM THE BEGINNING
IT CAME FROM YOUR HEART

GOD HEARD YOUR PRAYERS
WHEN YOU ASKED HIM ABOUT ME
FOR HIM NOT TO HEAR YOU
WOULD MAKE PRAYER MOCKERY

YES, MY DEAR SISTER
ON THIS DAY OF YOUR BIRTH
YOUR BIG BABY BROTHER
KNOWS WHAT YOU ARE WORTH

PEACE
by
Joseph Fram

I WANDER IN AND OUT OF LIFE
WITH REALLY NOTHING ON MY MIND
WHEN I GET TO WHERE I GO
I DON'T KNOW WHAT I FIND

I LOOK IT UP AND LOOK IT DOWN
DO I TAKE IT HOME TO KEEP?
MAYBE JUST A TASTE OF THIS AND THAT
BUT PLEASE, DON'T DISTURB MY SLEEP

EACH NEW DAY, EYES OPEN WIDE
I LET MY NEW SEARCH BEGIN
FOR EACH DAY IS CLEARED NOW
AND MAKING SENSE FROM DEEP WITHIN

I FIND MYSELF GOING HERE AND THERE
AND WHERE I AM IS FINE
I SPEND WHATEVER TIME I WANT
BECAUSE EACH MINUTE NOW IS MINE

IF YOU ARE BUSY, THAT'S O.K.
JUST LEAVE ME HERE IN PEACE
I AM CONTENT JUST WHERE I AM
I HOPE THIS FEELING WILL NOT CEASE

A LOOK AROUND
by
Joseph Fram

UNANCHORED SHIPS AT DOCK
SECURE IN CALM OF SEA
SLIGHT HINT OF A BREEZE
WONDER WHERE THEY WILL BE

PEACEFUL FROM INSIDE
TORNADO'S CENTER EYE
ALL AROUND IS LOST
SURVIVORS WONDER WHY

EARTH SPLITS THE GROUND
FEW PEOPLE ON THAT LAND
HOW THEY ALL ESCAPE
HARD TO UNDERSTAND

TORMENTED SOULS ALONE
THOUGH OTHERS ARE AROUND
THEY SELF PREDICT DESPAIR
THEY HEAR NO OTHER SOUND

MOST CURSE THE DAMAGE DONE
SHAKE THEIR FISTS INTO THE SKY
I CALMLY LOOK AROUND
AND TRY TO FIND OUT WHY

FIRST FORGIVE YOURSELF
by
Joseph Fram

I GUESS WE HAVE ALL BEEN ANGRY
THE REASONS MATTER NAUGHT
CHANCES ARE IT WAS THAT MOMENT
WHEN OFF GUARD WE WERE CAUGHT

BUT SOMETIMES IT STILL LINGERS
WE TRY TO FIGURE OUT WHY
IT JUST COMES AT ANY MOMENT
CAN'T LOSE IT IF WE TRY

THEN WE TRY FORGIVING
THE OTHER PARTY IN THE SCENES
WHEN IT DOESN'T HELP US INSIDE
WE ARE CLUELESS WHAT IT MEANS

A WISE MAN ONCE TOLD ME
YOU MUST BE PURE OF HEART
IF FORGIVENESS IS TO BE GIVEN
IN YOURSELF IS WHERE TO START

FIRST YOU MUST FORGIVE YOURSELF
FOR LETTING ANGER IN YOUR SOUL
THEN YOU BEGIN TO SLOWLY HEAL
UNTIL YOU ARE FINALLY WHOLE

SUDDEN END
by
Joseph Fram

IT TOOK YEARS OF MY LIFE
BEFORE LOVE CAME TO ME
THOUGH I WAS MARRIED FOREVER
TRUE LOVE COULDN'T BE

YES, I DID LOVE HER
BUT I WASN'T IN LOVE
FROM THE FIRST DAY WE MARRIED
IT WASN'T BLESSED FROM ABOVE

THEN WHEN I ASKED HER
TO COME TO THE ALTAR WITH ME
SHE THOUGHT IF GOD BLESSED US
SHE WOULD NO LONGER BE FREE

THEN I REMEMBERED
HOW LONG DID LOVE TAKE
NOT BEING TIED IN GOD'S EYES
A PERFECT UNION TO MAKE

THE REASON SHE GAVE ME
THERE'S ANOTHER MAN IN HER LIFE
THE YEARS THAT I LOVED HER
ENDED WHEN HE TOOK MY WIFE

NOT THERE
by
Joseph Fram

FOR THE FIRST TIME IN A LONG TIME
I DREAMED OF US LAST NIGHT
THERE WERE HOUSES AND STRANGERS
I KNEW SOMETHING WAS NOT RIGHT

THE HOUSE THAT WE HAD LIVED IN
YOU HAD CHANGED SO DRASTICALLY
I COULD TELL FROM ALL THE CHANGES
PLANS YOU MADE DID NOT INCLUDE ME

IN MY DREAM I TRIED TO ASK YOU
ABOUT YOUR NEW LIFE AND YOUR WAY
BUT I JUST DO NOT REMEMBER
IF YOU HAD ANYTHING TO SAY

THEN I TRIED TO PICTURE
OF THE WAY YOU USED TO LOOK
THEN A GESTURE THAT YOU MADE
WAS A FRIENDLY ONE I MISTOOK

THEN AS I AWAKENED
I FELT I JUST DIDN'T CARE
IN MY DREAMS I DO NOT SEE YOU
I GUESS YOU JUST DON'T BELONG THERE

DIGNITY
by
Joseph Fram

WHEN SHE LEFT SHE TOLD ME
SHE COULDN'T STAND TO KISS MY LIPS
SHE WOULD ALWAYS TURN AWAY
WHEN SHE FELT MY FINGER TIPS

EVERY TIME THAT WE MADE LOVE
INSIDE SHE STRUGGLED TO BE FREE
SHE SAID SHE WANTED TO MAKE LOVE
BUT WITH OTHERS, NOT WITH ME

SO SHE PLAYED THIS GAME OF HERS
HOPED THAT I WOULD NEVER KNOW
SHE UNWILLINGLY HELD MY HAND
AND NEVER ONCE TOLD ME TO GO

SHE LET ME THINK I WAS HER MAN
SHE EMBRACED WITHOUT A HEART
DID SHE NOT THINK I HAD SOME PRIDE
OR THAT WE COULD LIVE APART

COULD SHE NOT SEE IT WAS CRUEL
TO BE HELD BY ONE WHO DOESN'T CARE
OR THAT THE DIGNITY OF MAN
DOES NOT PERMIT HIM TO STAY THERE

ALMOST PASSED ME BY
by
Joseph Fram

TO THINK IT ALMOST PASSED ME BY
IN A STROLL OF LIFE SO UNPREPARED
NOT HAVING HAD I DIDN'T MISS
I HAD NO REASON TO BE SCARED

IT WAS ALWAYS IN MY MIND
SHE HAD NO TIME FOR SOUL AND HEART
AND I WOULD GUESS SHE FELT THE SAME
OH, HOW WELL WE PLAYED THE PART

YES WE LOVED, BUT NOT IN LOVE
THE LOVE THAT STANDS THE TEST OF TIME
ALL THE PASSION THAT WE SHARED
WE MISTOOK FOR LOVE SUBLIME

JUST TO LOVE WHEN NOT IN LOVE
WILL SLOWLY SLIP UNTIL THE FALL
FOR THIS IS LOVE YOU CANNOT MEND
THERE ARE NO STEPS TO CLIMB THIS WALL

IT TOOK SO LONG FOR ME TO KNOW
THAT IT ALMOST PASSED ME BY
I HAD TO GIVE UP ALL MY PAST
BUT I NEVER STOP TO QUESTION WHY

TURNING PAGES
by
Joseph Fram

I HAVE OFTEN LIKENED
MY LIFE UNTO A BOOK THAT'S READ
THRILLED BY PAGES I AM READING
TEMPTED TO TURN THE PAGE AHEAD

FOR I KNOW THE PAGE I'M ON
MUST END BEFORE I TURN
HOPE I ONLY READ IT ONCE
FROM IT THAT I WILL LEARN

SOMETIMES THERE ARE PAGES
I READ AND THEN READ AGAIN
SOME OF THEM BRING HAPPINESS
SOME OF THEM BRING PAIN

YET I KEEP ON READING
I DARE NOT PUT THIS BOOK AWAY
EVERYTHING I AM IS THERE
WHEN I LEAVE THE BOOK WILL STAY

ONE THING THAT I KNOW NOW
AT LONG LAST I HAVE LEARNED
ONE CANNOT ADVANCE THE PAGE
UNTIL THE PAGE THEY'RE ON IS TURNED

RIGHT SIDE UP
by
Joseph Fram

I HADN'T HEARD THAT VOICE OF HERS
SINCE THE TIME WE SAID GOODBYE
MANY YEARS HAD PASSED SINCE THEN
I HAD NO OCCASION TO WONDER WHY

ALL THE STRINGS THAT TIED US DOWN
WERE GONE WHEN WE PARTED ON THAT DAY
THEN OUR PATHS WOULD NEVER CROSS
AS WE EACH WENT OUR SEPARATE WAY

I WAS SEARCHING BUT COULDN'T FIND
HAPPINESS WE MIGHT HAVE SHARED
BUT I THOUGHT THERE MUST HAVE BEEN
AT A TIME WHEN WE STILL CARED

WHEN SHE TURNED MY WORLD UPSIDE DOWN
I HAD GIVEN MORE THAN I COULD GIVE
I HAD KEPT THAT PART OF ME
THAT HAS THE WILL TO LIVE

WHEN SHE CALLED THE OTHER DAY
THERE WAS NO BEATING OF MY HEART
I HAD HOPED HER DOING WELL
AND I'M RIGHT SIDE UP SINCE WE'RE APART

BLOOMSDAY SPOKANE
by
Joseph Fram

I FINALLY DID THAT BLOOMSDAY
ALTHOUGH MY TIME WAS NOT TOO GOOD
BUT WHEN I STOP TO THINK OF IT
I NEVER REALLY THOUGHT I WOULD

IT HAD ALWAYS BEEN SO EASY
TO LET BLOOMSDAY PASS ON BY
WHEN I DIDN'T JOIN THAT YEAR
IN RETROSPECT I'D WONDER WHY

BUT THIS YEAR IT WAS EASY
I HAD A FRIEND TO GO WITH ME
DOING THE RACE BY YOURSELF
IS NOT THE WAY TO BE

WE BOTH HAD SUCH A GLORIOUS TIME
AS WE PASSED EACH MILE HAND IN HAND
SIXTY THOUSAND MARCHED WITH US
TO MAKE THE BIGGEST BRASS-LESS BAND

WHEN WE CROSSED THE FINISH LINE
WE WERE TIRED FOR A WHILE
WHEN WE KNEW WHAT WE HAD DONE
THE PAIN BECAME A VICTORY SMILE

FIRST LOVE
by
Joseph Fram

I KEEP KNOCKING ON EACH DOOR
LOOKING FOR WHAT I CANNOT FIND
EACH TIME I GET A RESPONSE
IT IS WRONG BUT MOSTLY KIND

I LOOK INTO SEARCHING EYES
IN OTHERS LOOKING FOR THEIR PAST
ALTHOUGH THEY THOUGHT THEY KNEW ME
THE SHORT VISIT COULD NEVER LAST

MY LIFE HAD BEEN UPROOTED
MY FOREVER HAD AN END
WHEN I TRIED A NEW FOREVER
I HAD ONLY FOUND A FRIEND

THE SEARCH GOES ON FOR ALL OF US
EACH NEW DOOR SEEMS THE SAME
EACH NEW FACE IS BRIGHT AND SHINY
BUT SOMEHOW I MISS THE NAME

I THINK WHEN WE WERE PUT ON EARTH
THE FIRST LOVE IS ALL WE SEE
I ALSO THINK MY SEARCH WILL END
WHEN MY FIRST LOVE BEGINS WITH ME

GOD IT IS FOR YOU
by
Joseph Fram

TEMPTATIONS HAVE BEEN AROUND ME
I SUSPECT SINCE I WAS A CHILD
I GUESS SATAN PUT IT BEFORE ME
TO SEE IF HE COULD DRIVE ME WILD

ALL THE SINS WERE SHOWN ME
HE TOLD ME THEY WERE GOOD
AND I WOULD BE SO HAPPY
IF ONLY THAT I WOULD

I DO ADMIT IT LOOKED SO NICE
THAT I SOMETIMES HAD TO SWAY
BUT JUST BEFORE I COMMIT THE SIN
I ASKED GOD "TAKE IT AWAY"

OTHERS HAD MUCH MORE THAN ME
PERHAPS SATAN HAD A HAND
I COULD NOT BRING MYSELF TO ENVY
NOR DID I TRY TO UNDERSTAND

I HAD LEARNED TO HANDLE IT
I KNOW EXACTLY WHAT TO DO
WHEN SATAN KNOCKS AT MY DOOR
I SAY "GOD IT IS FOR YOU"

ALL THE GIFTS OF CHRISTMAS
by
Joseph Fram

ALL THE GIFTS OF CHRISTMAS
SIT THERE WHERE I CAN SEE
NOT IN THE FORM OF PRESENTS
OR WHAT IS FOUND UNDER THE TREE

THE GIFTS I HAVE BEEN GIVEN
DID NOT COME ON CHRISTMAS DAY
THEY WERE GIVEN TO ME LONG AGO
AND THEY CAME FROM FAR AWAY

THEY ARE GIFTS I DEARLY CHERISH
I SEE THEM CLEARLY IN MY MIND
THEY WERE GIVEN BY MY FRIENDS
WHEN I NEEDED SOMEONE KIND

I HAVE THE GIFT OF FAMILY
WHERE LOVE FLOWS TO AND FRO
A GIFT I KNOW IS ALWAYS THERE
MAKES NO MATTER WHERE I GO

A SPECIAL GIFT I HAVE FROM GOD
WHO WAS WITH ME FROM THE START
A GIFT THAT I SHALL NEVER LOSE
HE PLACED LOVE INTO MY HEART

19

FLYING BY
by
Joseph Fram

I WATCHED THE PLANES GO FLYING BY
TO SCURRY FROM HERE TO YON
A NEW FACE EACH DAY IN EVERY SEAT
HALF WONDERING WHY THEY'VE GONE

IT IS SO IMPORTANT THAT WE MEET
TIME IS OF THE ESSENCE NOW
BE SURE YOU CATCH THE FIRST PLANE
WE MUST COMPLETE OUR PLANS SOMEHOW

DID I FORGET OR DID I NOT
YESTERDAY OUR PLAN WAS GREAT
NOW YOU SAY THAT WE MUST CHANGE
THE NEW PLAN JUST CANNOT WAIT

AS THE PLANES GO FLYING BY
WITH THE WORLD IN SUCH A HURRY
THERE MUST BE SOMETHING WRONG WITH ME
BECAUSE I NEVER SEEM TO WORRY

WELL, MAYBE EVERY NOW AND THEN
I TURN IT UP A NOTCH OR TWO
THEN I REMEMBER NATURE'S PLAN
WHAT I FORGET, THE OTHERS DO

FRIENDSHIP
by
Joseph Fram

I CHANCED UPON A LONG LOST FRIEND
WITH WHOM I USED TO PLAY
WE'D SHARED A CHILDHOOD FULL OF FUN
BUT THEN I SOMEHOW WENT AWAY

FIRST WE SPOKE, THEN WE EMBRACED
TOLD EACH OTHER WE STILL CARED
A TOUCH OF SADNESS FILLED MY HEART
I MISSED THE TIMES WE DIDN'T SHARE

CHILDHOOD DREAMS WE SHARED WERE LOST
MEMORIES OF YOUTH WERE GONE
THROUGH A BARREN LAPSE OF TIME
CHILDHOOD FRIENDSHIP STILL LIVED ON

OH, WE ASKED WHAT WE HAD DONE
HOW OUR LIVES BROUGHT US TO BE
LOSING TOUCH WAS SUCH A WASTE
TIME ELAPSED WITHOUT A MEMORY

IT WAS GOOD TO SEE MY FRIEND
THOUGH SEPARATION LEFT A VOID
WHEN I THINK OF ALL I MISSED
FRIENDSHIP LOST LEAVES ME ANNOYED

TATTERED MEMORIES
by
Joseph Fram

YOU KNOW WE STAYED TOGETHER
FOR SUCH A LONG, LONG TIME
BUT YOU NEVER SHARED YOUR TRUE LOVE
ALTHOUGH I GAVE YOU ALL OF MINE

THOUGH WE STAYED TOGETHER
I NEVER KNEW YOU WERE UNTRUE
I JUST KEPT BUILDING MEMORIES
THAT SOMEDAY I WOULD SHARE WITH YOU

THOSE MEMORIES WERE PRECIOUS THEN
BECAUSE THEY LIVED INSIDE MY HEART
WHEN YOU LOVED ANOTHER MAN
MY PRECIOUS MEMORIES HAD NO PART

AFTER ALL THAT TIME WITH YOU
YOU'D THINK SOME TENDERNESS I'D SEE
WHEN YOU BROKE YOUR TRUST THAT DAY
YOU DIDN'T LEAVE ONE HAPPY MEMORY

THE MEMORIES I WAS BUILDING
I THOUGHT YOU AND I COULD SHARE
BUT THE MEMORIES THAT YOU WANTED
WERE BUILT FOR YOU ELSEWHERE

GROWING YOUNG
by
Joseph Fram

I THOUGHT MY LIFE WAS OVER
THE DAY SHE WALKED OUT ON ME
THE AGING I WAS DOING
WAS ONE I COULD NOT SEE

WE WERE GROWING OLD TOGETHER
A STATE OF MIND I FELL INTO
WITH BUT DEATH TO WELCOME ME
I HAD NOTHING BETTER THEN TO DO

WHEN SHE LEFT I CAME ALIVE
I WAS A BOY AND YOUNG AGAIN
I TOOK SOME TIME TO FEEL THIS WAY
YES, I DID GO THROUGH SOME PAIN

NOW I LOOK BACK AT MY LIFE
I DON'T REGRET THE THINGS I'VE DONE
I'LL LEAVE MY HISTORY AS IT IS
AND CLEAR THE WAY TO HAVE SOME FUN

I FEEL A FUN-LOVING YOUTH
WANTS TO USE MY BODY FOR A WHILE
PERHAPS HE HAS BEEN THERE ALL THE TIME
SO I WILL JUST ENJOY AND SMILE

THY WILL BE DONE
by
Joseph Fram

EACH DAY MY PRAYER
IS THAT I WILL BE
A LITTLE BIT MORE LIKE
WHAT GOD WOULD LIKE TO SEE

TO FOLLOW MY DREAM
WITH MY HONOR INTACT
KNOW I HAVE DONE RIGHT
NOT HAVING TO LOOK BACK

WHEN OTHERS TELL ME
IT IS TIME TO MOVE ON
I HOPE IT IS THE REAL ME
THAT GREETS THE NEW DAWN

AS FOR ALL OF THE OTHERS
I WISH THEM PEACE IN EVERY WAY
IF THEY FOLLOW THEIR HEART'S PATH
WHAT MORE IS THERE TO SAY

WHEN I AWAKE EACH MORNING
AND MY PRAYER HAS BEGUN
BY ASKING FOR HIS BLESSING
AND THAT HIS WILL BE DONE

PICTURES IN MY MIND
by
Joseph Fram

IN MY MIND THERE ARE PICTURES
OF THE WAY THINGS OUGHT TO BE
HANDSOME KNIGHTS AND MAIDENS FAIR
IN MY MIND, ONE OF THEM IS ME

ALL IS FAIR, I LIKE TO THINK
TRUE LOVE WILL NEVER DIE
AND ALL THE LABORS OF MY LOVE
WILL NEVER BE A LIE

I SEE MYSELF THROUGH MY OWN EYES
BUT WHAT DO OTHERS SEE
I LIKE TO THINK WHAT'S IN MY MIND
IS WHAT I WILL ALWAYS BE

THEN THERE ARE THE OTHERS
TO UPSET THE PICTURES IN MY MIND
I TRY TO GENTLY PUSH THEM OUT
AND NOT TO SEEM UNKIND

IF IT'S REAL OR IF IT'S NOT
DOESN'T LIFE GO ON AND ON
I'LL KEEP THOSE PICTURES IN MY MIND
WITH HOPES THAT THEY ARE NEVER GONE

LOVE BETRAYED
by
Joseph Fram

A LOVE BETRAYED
CAN NEVER DIE
IT WILL ALWAYS LIVE
IN HEARTS THAT LIE

WHEN ONE YOU TRUST
BETRAYS ALL THAT IS TRUE
THAT LOVE BETRAYED
WILL ALWAYS STAY NEW

FOR DAY TO DAY
THE BETRAYAL COMES TO MIND
THERE IS NOWHERE TO RUN
AND NO PEACE CAN YOU FIND

YOU MAY SEE CHANGE OUTSIDE
BUT NOT IN YOUR HEART
THE LOVE THAT'S BETRAYED
WILL NOT LET GUILT PART

LOVE OLD OR NEW
IT IS ALL JUST THE SAME
WHEN A LOVE IS BETRAYED
BY ANY OTHER NAME

BEST FRIEND
by
Joseph Fram

WE RUN AWAY TILL WE FIND OURSELVES
IT SEEMS OUR SEARCH WILL NEVER END
THE PEACE WE SEEK WE ALWAYS LOSE
A RUNNING HEART WILL NEVER MEND

WE BUILD OUR HOPE ON SOMEONE ELSE
AND TRY TO LIVE THE LIFE THEY CHOOSE
THOUGH WE TRY OUR BEST TO PLEASE
IN THE END WE ALWAYS LOSE

WE LOOK TO OTHERS FOR THEIR PRAISE
SELDOM GIVE ANY OF OUR OWN
WHAT THEY SAY SOON MATTERS NOT
WHEN THEY LEAVE US ALL ALONE

WE NEVER KNOW WHO FRIENDS ARE
THOUGH WE TRY TO MAKE THEM EVERY DAY
JUST WHEN WE THINK WE HAVE ONE
THEY SOMEHOW SLIP AWAY

THEN ONE DAY WE LOOK WITHIN
OUR RUNNING DAYS ARE AT AN END
WE KEEP THE GOOD AND LOSE THE BAD
WHEN WE BECOME OUR OWN BEST FRIEND

HILLS
by
Joseph Fram

A JOYFUL TIME A SUDDEN CRASH
SUDDENLY LIFE IS NOT THE SAME
FOR IN THE BLINKING OF AN EYE
YOU'RE IN A WHOLE NEW GAME

THE LIFE YOU KNEW NOT LONG AGO
SEEMS LIKE A DREAM SOMEHOW
WHAT MATTERED SO JUST YESTERDAY
HAS LOST ITS URGENCY FOR NOW

THE DREAMS WE HAD WHEN WE WERE STRONG
WOULD CARRY US WITHOUT A DOUBT
BUT SUDDENLY WE ARE WEAK
WE CANNOT FIND A WAY OUT

PERHAPS THOSE HILLS WE CHOSE TO CLIMB
WENT FAR BEYOND OUR SKILL
OR ALL THE ROADBLOCKS IN THE CLIMB
WERE PUT THERE BY OUR WILL

NOW WE GAZE INTO EACH OTHERS' EYES
WE KNOW, THOUGH NO ONE SPEAKS
WE CLIMBED SOME HILLS WAY BACK THEN
BUT WE NEVER REACHED THE PEAKS

TILL THEY ARE ALL GONE
by
Joseph Fram

HAPPY BIRTHDAY MY SWEET DOREEN
HERE WE ARE, ONE MORE YEAR
I AM SO HAPPY WE CAN SHARE
ALL THOSE THINGS THAT WE HOLD DEAR

YOU ARE THE SAME TO ME TODAY
AS YOU WERE WHEN WE FIRST MET
WHEN I TOOK YOUR HAND IN MINE
THERE IS NO WAY I CAN FORGET

THOUGH AGE HAS TOUCHED OUR BODIES
IT CANNOT ERASE OUR LOVE OF YOUTH
FOR LOVE CANNOT GROW OLD
WHEN IT IS GIVEN YOU IN TRUTH

EACH BIRTHDAY THAT WE SEE
BRINGS YOU CLOSER IN MY MIND
THERE IS NO OTHER THAT I KNOW
THAT TO ME HAS BEEN SO KIND

WITH EACH BIRTHDAY
YOU HAVE FROM NOW ON
I WILL SHARE THEM WITH YOU
TILL THEY ARE ALL GONE

I AM SPECIAL
by
Joseph Fram

I HAVE ALWAYS KNOWN I AM SPECIAL
FROM MY HEAD DOWN TO MY TOES
FOR GOD IS ALWAYS WITH ME
FOR WHERE I GO HE GOES

SOME MAY TRY TO PUT ME DOWN
THEY TELL ME I'M NOT SMART
I'LL BET WHY THEY DO THAT
GOD IS NOT INTO THEIR HEART

OTHERS TRY TO PREVENT ME
FROM REACHING GOALS THAT I HAVE SET
WHEN I HAVE PROVED MYSELF
HOW VERY QUICKLY THEY FORGET

THEN THERE ARE THOSE WITH STANDARDS
TOO LOW FOR ME TO LIVE
WHEN THEY TRY TO PULL ME DOWN
MY HIGHER STANDARDS DO I GIVE

BECAUSE I MAKE MYSELF SO SPECIAL
I LET THE WORLD THINK WHAT THEY MAY
AND I PRAY THAT THEIR TOMORROW
LETS THEM FEEL LIKE ME TODAY

SCARS DON'T DISAPPEAR
by
Joseph Fram

WHEN YOU TRUST ANOTHER WITH YOUR LOVE
THAT TRUST SHOULD LAST FOREVER
IT IS ONE SHOULD SEE YOU THROUGH
THEN, NOW, AND THE TWELFTH OF NEVER

THERE IS NOTHING MORE TO GIVE
ONCE LOVE IS GIVEN FROM THE HEART
IT SHOULD STAY BETWEEN THE TWO
UNTIL THE TIME DEATH DO US PART

WHEN ONE CASTS THAT LOVE ASIDE
THEY MAY WANDER NEAR OR FAR
LIFE MAY CHANGE FOR GOOD OR BAD
THEY WILL ALWAYS WEAR THAT SCAR

ONE WILL ALWAYS WONDER WHY
THOUGH IT REALLY MATTERS NOT
IT'S TRUE THAT LIFE GOES ON
BUT GIVEN LOVE IS NOT FORGOT

WHEN YOU GAVE THAT LOVE AWAY
IT WAS ALL THAT YOU HELD DEAR
IT WOULD BE A SINFUL THING
IF SCARS LIKE THAT WOULD DISAPPEAR

SECOND CHANCE
by
Joseph Fram

ONCE UPON A DREAM
AND IT HAPPENED NOT SO LONG AGO
AN OLD LOVE HAD A SECOND CHANCE
TO SPARK AND MAYBE GROW

IT WAS LIKE MY SWEETEST DREAM
WITH LOVE FROM DARK TILL MORNING LIGHT
WHEN OUR LIPS TOUCHED TIME REVERSED
NOW BACK TOGETHER ALL WAS RIGHT

A SECOND CHANCE AT AN OLD LOVE
IT COULD HAPPEN ONLY IN A DREAM
BUT THERE WE WERE IN SWEET EMBRACE
IN LOVE'S MOST PRECIOUS GLEAM

IT HAD TO BE A FANTASY
A GIFT FROM UP ABOVE
FOR ONCE IN EVERY CREATURE'S LIFE
GOD SENDS SOMEONE TO LOVE

BUT ALAS, IT WAS BUT A DREAM
MY SECOND CHANCE WENT UP IN AIR
WHEN I REACHED TO TOUCH HER FACE
I REACHED BUT SHE WASN'T THERE

WHEN LOVE IS REAL
by
Joseph Fram

LOVE IS A WORD
THAT IS THROWN AROUND
BUT HOW OFTEN
IS IT EVER FOUND

IT SEEMS EASY TO LOVE
WHEN ALL IS JUST RIGHT
WHEN THE GOALS OF NEW LOVE
ARE STILL IN YOUR SIGHT

BUT THE REAL TEST OF LOVE
IS WHEN SOMETHING GOES WRONG
LIKE AN ILLNESS OR ISSUE
THAT DOES NOT BELONG

WHEN YOU SEE SOMEONE YOU LOVE
CHANGE BEFORE YOUR VERY EYES
YOU KNOW THEN AND THERE
IS IT TRUE LOVE OR LIES

WHEN YOUR LOVE IS FOR REAL
AND YOU SEE THE OTHER'S INSIDE
THE BEAUTY THAT HAS BOUND YOU
WILL NOT LET YOUR LOVE HIDE

FEELINGS
by
Joseph Fram

THEY ARE FEELINGS THAT I HAVE
EVERY NOW AND THEN
I HAVE THEM FOR A LITTLE WHILE
THEN I'M MYSELF AGAIN

I REALLY LIKE THE WAY I AM
BUT FEELINGS ARE ALWAYS THERE
I NEVER KNOW JUST HOW I'LL FEEL
AND CERTAINLY DON'T KNOW WHERE

SOMETIMES THERE'S A FEEL OF LOVE
IN AN EXTRAORDINARY PLACE
IT COMES FROM A TOUCH OF HAND
OR FROM A LONG-LOST FACE

HATE COMES ONCE IN A WHILE
SOMETIMES IT TRIES TO STAY
WHEN I POUR SOME LOVE ON IT
THEN THAT FEELING GOES AWAY

YES, THEY ARE ONLY FEELINGS
AND ONLY PASSING THROUGH
IF I TRUST MY FEELINGS
I KNOW JUST WHAT TO DO

GOING BACK
by
Joseph Fram

THE SOUNDS AND SMELLS OF CHILDHOOD
TAKE ME BACK TO A JOYFUL TIME
WHEN EVERYTHING WAS NEW TO ME
AND ALL THE WORLD WAS MINE

A TIME WHEN TIME WAS ON MY SIDE
I HAD TIME TO RUN AND PLAY
AND ALL THE THINGS THAT OTHERS DID
I PUT OFF FOR ANOTHER DAY

A TIME WHEN I HAD TIME TO DREAM
MY WORLD WAS IN MY MIND
AND EVERY PLACE WAS A SURPRISE
NEVER KNOWING WHAT I'D FIND

WHEN OTHERS TRIED TO TELL ME
JUST HOW THE WORLD SHOULD BE
IT WAS A TIME THAT I KNEW INSIDE
THEY LOOKED BUT COULD NOT SEE

NOW IT IS TIME TO SHED THIS TIME
I'VE SEEN THE WORLD AS OTHERS DID
I'LL PUT AWAY ALL THE GROWN-UP THINGS
AND BRING BACK THE TIME I WAS A KID

A MOMENT SHARED
by
Joseph Fram

SOMETIMES IT JUST HAPPENS
A FRIEND YOU'VE NEVER MET
YOU CAN SHARE A MOMENT
THAT NEITHER WILL FORGET

AT TIMES LIKE THIS I ONLY HOPE
I AM MY TRUE SELF FOR THE DAY
FOR I WOULD LIKE THEM FOR A FRIEND
BEFORE THEY GO THEIR WAY

THERE ARE MANY PARTS OF ME
THE GOOD ONES SHOULD NOT HIDE
I HOPE THAT WHAT'S THE WORST OF ME
FOR THE MOMENT STAYS INSIDE

I WOULD LIKE TO SHARE MY LOVE
AND LET MY NEW FRIEND PASS IT ON
FOR LOVE IS ALL THAT I CAN LEAVE
ONCE MY LIFE ON EARTH IS GONE

SO WHEN I MEET A STRANGER
I PRAY THEY LEAVE AS A FRIEND
IF A BIT OF LOVE IS SHARED
PERHAPS THAT CHAIN WILL NEVER END

YOU LOSE
by
Joseph Fram

A MEMORY IS A JOURNEY'S MAP
ONE THAT IS NOT COMPLETED YET
IT IS MEANT TO LEAD YOU TO YOUR GOAL
AND TO LET YOU NOT FORGET

AS YOU TRAVEL FROM THE PAST
YOUR LIFE IS MEANT TO GROW
TRAVELING THOSE OLD ROADS AGAIN
MAKES YOUR JOURNEY AWFUL SLOW

THERE YOU SEE THINGS YOU'VE SEEN
AND SOME MISTAKES YOU'VE MADE
WHEN YOU TRY TO CORRECT THEM
YOU PAY BILLS THAT HAVE BEEN PAID

ALL THE THINGS YOU HAVE DONE
YOU CANNOT CORRECT FROM NOW
JUST MARK THE SPOT ON YOUR MAP
AND LEARN FROM IT SOMEHOW

SO WHEN YOU LOOK UPON YOUR MAP
TAKE CARE THE ROUTE YOU CHOOSE
SOME DEAD END MEMORIES WAIT FOR YOU
DON'T TAKE THEM OR YOU LOSE

WATCHING SOMEONE DIE
by
Joseph Fram

WATCHING SOME DIE
IS NOT A VERY PLEASANT THING
EVERY DAY YOU WATCH IT
MORE DEPRESSION DOES IT BRING

YOU TRY TO DO ALL THAT YOU CAN
TO MAKE THE SITUATION RIGHT
HOW LITTLE YOU MAKE PROGRESS
WILL HIT YOU LATE AT NIGHT

SHE IS THE ONE THAT YOU LOVE
YOU HOPE FOR SOMETHING GOOD
THAT SHE IS NOT COMING BACK
IS NOT QUITE UNDERSTOOD

YOUR PRAYERS FOR HER MAY HELP
YOU ASK GOD TO GIVE SOME AID
SHE DOESN'T GET ANY BETTER
NO MATTER HOW YOU PRAYED

YOU JUST HAVE TO TURN IT OVER
TO YOUR GOD TO DO HIS DEED
HE WILL DO THE RIGHT THING
AT THE TIME HE SEES THE NEED

TOUCH OF LOVE
by
Joseph Fram

WHEN SHE PUTS HER HAND IN MINE
I KNOW MY WORLD IS RIGHT
FOR IT HAS THAT FEEL OF LOVE
NO MATTER DAY OR NIGHT

IT'S THE TOUCH THAT BRINGS ME CALM
THAT TELLS ME THAT SHE CARES
ONE THAT SOOTHES WHATEVER PAIN
AND WHATEVER JOY IT SHARES

TO LET ME KNOW SHE NEED NOT SPEAK
HER TOUCH SAYS ALL THAT I SHOULD KNOW
SHE MAKES ME TINGLE ALL INSIDE
AND SILENTLY BEGS TO NOT LET GO

IT IS A TOUCH THAT SAYS I'M YOURS
I WILL BE HERE UNTIL THE END
YOU WILL ALWAYS HAVE THIS TOUCH
BOTH AS A LOVER AND A FRIEND

YES, THIS TOUCH IS OURS ALONE
NO OTHER TOUCH CAN FEEL THIS WAY
THIS TOUCH OF LOVE WILL ALWAYS BE
AND I WILL LOVE HER COME WHAT MAY

ON CHRISTMAS DAY
by
Joseph Fram

ON CHRISTMAS DAY, IN A CHURCH
THERE ALONE SITS AN OLD MAN
THE THOUGHTS OF CHRISTMAS PAST
THROUGH HIS MIND RAN

HIS THOUGHTS WANDERED
TO A LONG TIME AGO
WHEN HIS FATHER HAD LEFT HIM
IT WAS TO HEAVEN I KNOW

FOR HE WAS A CHILD
THERE WAS NAUGHT HE COULD DO
HIS MOTHER WAS GONE
HE FELT ALONE TOO

THEN HE THOUGHT OF HIS HOME
WHERE HE WATCHED CHILDREN GROW
BUT THAT IS GONE ALSO
HE HAS NOTHING TO SHOW

SO ALONE IN A CHURCH
THESE ARE MEMORIES HE KEEPS
ALL HE HAS IS THE MEMORIES
SO HE SITS THERE AND WEEPS

HURTING PART OF LOVE
by
Joseph Fram

I HAVE HAD THE HURTING PART OF LOVE
AND IT CHANGED MY LIFE A BIT
ALL THE HURTS YOU PUT ON ME
MADE OTHER LOVING NOT QUITE FIT

ALL THE THINGS WE DID TOGETHER
ALWAYS WERE OURS JUST ALONE
OUR DREAMS WE PUT IN A PACKAGE
THAT PACKAGE WAS OUR HOME

YOU DIDN'T WANT TO STAY THERE
YOU SAID THE PACKAGE WAS TOO SMALL
ALL THE PROMISES THAT YOU MADE ME
WAS THE HURTING PART MOST OF ALL

NOW YOU TELL IT'S QUITE COMMON
HURTING LOVE IS JUST A GAME
NO MATTER WHERE I GO NOW
IT WILL ALWAYS BE THE SAME

IF THE HURTING PART OF LOVING
COMES WITH EACH NEW ROMANCE
I'LL JUST STAY HERE ALL ALONE
I DON'T THINK I WANT ANOTHER CHANCE

MY DAUGHTER DANA
by
Joseph Fram

I WILL ALWAYS LOVE SEATTLE
IT WAS THERE WHERE YOU WERE BORN
YOU JUST COULDN'T WAIT FOR MAY
SO YOU CAME ONE APRIL MORN

YOU WERE MY FIRST BORN CHILD
BORN IN LOVE RIGHT FROM THE START
AS I WATCHED YOU GROW UP
I SAW THE KINDNESS IN YOUR HEART

I STILL SEE THE LITTLE GIRL
RUN AND GREET ME ON OUR LAWN
I REACH BACK IN TIME TO PICK YOU UP
BUT FIND THAT LITTLE GIRL IS GONE

I WAS THERE THROUGHOUT THE YEARS
TO SEE YOU GROW IN LOVE AND GRACE
AND I HOPE YOU KNOW BY NOW
NO ONE COULD EVER TAKE YOUR PLACE

WHEN OTHERS SPEAK OF CHILDHOOD
I TELL THEM "WHAT MORE COULD I ASK"
TO BRING UP A DAUGHTER JUST LIKE YOU
GOD GAVE ME LIFE'S MOST EASY TASK

REQUIEM
by
Joseph Fram

HE LETS US HAVE THEM FOR A WHILE
THEY FILL OUR LIVES WITH FUN
WHEN THEY PASS OUT OF OUR LIVES
HE'S THERE TO SEND ANOTHER ONE

WE CAN ONLY STAY ON EARTH
TILL WHAT WE MUST DO IS O'ER
IF WE DO IT WELL ENOUGH
HE WILL NEVER ASK FOR MORE

THERE IS PAIN WHEN THEY DEPART
IT CAN'T BE ANY OTHER WAY
THE PAIN WE FEEL SHOWS WE CARE
BUT THEY WERE NEVER HERE TO STAY

SOMETIMES SOMEONE ELSE WILL SHARE
A PAIN YOU THOUGHT MADE ONLY FOR YOU
HE HAS TAKEN OTHER LIVES
THEIR WORK ON EARTH WAS THROUGH

HE LETS US HAVE THEM FOR A WHILE
TO SHARE A LOVE THAT'S JUST THE SAME
WHEN ALL OUR LOVE AND PAIN ARE GONE
HE HAS CALLED US BY OUR NAME

OH! MY SCIATICA
by
Joseph Fram

WHOA, WHAT IS THAT PAIN
THAT RUNS DOWN MY LEG
A PAIN SO POWERFUL IN STRENGTH
IT CAN CAUSE ONE TO BEG

THE PAIN REMAINS WITH YOU
ALL DAY AND ALL NIGHT
YOU CAN'T GET AWAY
THERE IS NO USE TO FIGHT

IT WILL GRIND YOU DOWN
YOU NO LONGER WANT TO LIVE
IF THE PAIN JUST GOES AWAY
EVERYTHING YOU WILL GIVE

YOU GO TO THE DOCTOR
THEN YOU BEG AND YOU PLEAD
MAKE THE PAIN STOP
IS THE ONE THING I NEED

WHEN THE OPERATION IS OVER
FINALLY THERE IS NO MORE PAIN
YOU FALL TO YOUR KNEES
YOU CAN LIVE ONCE AGAIN

CANNOT ERASE
by
Joseph Fram

A ROAD NEVER TAKEN
A THOUGHT NEVER SAID
A TUNE NEVER PLAYED
A BOOK NEVER READ

IN OUR WEARY JOURNEY
OUR LIFE WILL GO ON
WORRY IS FOR NAUGHT
SOON WE WILL BE GONE

HOW DOES IT MATTER
WHAT DIFFERENCE CAN IT MAKE
IT IS WHAT WE LEAVE BEHIND
NOT WHAT WE WILL TAKE

LIFE IS OF CHOICES
AROUND EVERY TURN
FOR EACH OF THOSE CHOICES
LET US PRAY THAT WE LEARN

I WILL KEEP ON SEARCHING
TILL I FIND MY PLACE
I PUT EACH DAY BEHIND ME
IN A LIFE NO ONE CAN ERASE

GOD'S PLAN
by
Joseph Fram

I KNOW GOD SENT HER TO MY SIDE
A MORTAL WOUND TO HEAL
THERE WERE OTHERS THERE TO HELP
BUT GOD'S HANDS THROUGH HERS I'D FEEL

SHE TOOK ME THROUGH MY DARKEST TIME
WAS THERE WHEN ALL WAS LOST
SHE STOPPED THE BLEEDING IN MY HEART
AND NEVER STOPPED TO ASK THE COST

WHEN I WOULD TRY TO SLIP AWAY
AT NIGHT WHEN SHE WASN'T THERE
GOD PUT HER VOICE IN MY WAITING EAR
TO LET ME KNOW THAT SHE DID CARE

IT MUST HAVE BEEN A HUNDRED YEARS
THAT SHE HAD TO HOLD MY HAND
MY HURT WAS SO FAR DEEP WITHIN
AND WHY I COULD NOT UNDERSTAND

I DON'T QUESTION GOD'S GREAT PLAN
OR WHY A WIFE THAT WAS UNTRUE
FOR I WOULD NOT HAVE SEEN HIS FACE
AND KNOWN THE THINGS THAT HE CAN DO

YOU NEVER KNOW LOVE
by
Joseph Fram

YOU NEVER REALLY KNOW LOVE
UNTIL IT IS REACHING FOR ITS END
IT HAS ALWAYS BEEN THERE
BUT TRUE OR JUST A FRIEND?

WHEN SOMEONE IS NEAR THEIR END
AND YOU LOOK INTO THEIR EYES
THEN YOU CAN TELL REAL LOVE
THEY HAVEN'T TIME FOR LIES

THEY EXTEND THEIR HAND IN KINDNESS
JUST WANT TO FEEL YOUR TOUCH
AND HOLD YOU OH SO TENDERLY
THEY NEVER ASK FOR MUCH

THEY THANK YOU FOR BEING THERE
PRAY THAT YOU WILL STAY
TO BE WITH THEM UNTIL THE END
BEFORE THEY HAVE TO GO AWAY

THEY DO NOT WISH YOU SADNESS
THEY WISH THEY COULD DO MORE
THE PRAYERS YOU SAY TOGETHER
ARE FOR WHAT GOD HAS GOT IN STORE

REMEMBERING
by
Joseph Fram

I CANNOT REMEMBER
WHO IT WAS THAT HURT ME SO
OR IF IT WAS JUST YESTERDAY
COULD IT BE SOME TIME AGO?

I REMEMBER HAVING FEELINGS
AT TIMES THAT MADE ME MAD
I DON'T REMEMBER WHERE OR WHEN
FOR THIS, I AM ETERNALLY GLAD

I REMEMBER SOMEONE LEFT ME
WHEN I THOUGHT THAT THEY SHOULD STAY
I DON'T REMEMBER IF I SAID I'M SORRY
THAT THEY CHOSE TO GO AWAY

THOSE THINGS THAT I REMEMBER
CREEP SLOWLY FROM MY MIND
WHAT I CANNOT REMEMBER
I TRY HARD NOT TO FIND

REMEMBERING IS A FUNNY THING
SOMETIMES IT SERVES YOU WELL
I TRY TO LEAVE WELL ENOUGH ALONE
FOR SOME MEMORIES BRING YOU HELL

KNOW MY HEART
by
Joseph Fram

COULD I BUT KNOW MY ACHING HEART
MY LIFE WOULD CHANGE TODAY
I WOULD KNOW JUST WHERE IT IS
TO BRING HOME OR GIVE AWAY

MY RESTLESS HEART JUST WANDERS
IT LEAVES MY MIND AT HOME TO CRY
WHILE MY MIND SEARCHES FOR PEACE
MY RESTLESS HEART WON'T EVEN TRY

MY HEART ONCE LET MY MIND CONTROL
FOR YEARS IT DID NOT BEND
MY MIND COULD LIVE WITHOUT TRUE LOVE
NOW MY HEART THINKS THIS MUST END

MY MIND IS LIKE A SPINNING TOP
WHILE MY HEART DOES MANY THINGS
IT REACHES OUT TO ALL WHO CARE
IN HOPES THAT LOVE WITH THEM IT BRINGS

MY LIFE CHANGED WHEN SHE WALKED OUT
MY MIND KNOWS NOT WHERE TO START
IT WOULD BRING BACK LIFE TO ME
COULD I BUT KNOW MY HEART

PEACE BEFORE I DIE
by
Joseph Fram

I CAN'T LET GO OF EVERYTHING
ALTHOUGH MY LIFE DID CHANGE
FOR CHANGING ALL I USED TO BE
LEAVES ME FEELING SOMEWHAT STRANGE

THE FIRE OF MY YOUNGER DAYS
HAS TURNED FROM FLAME TO AMBER
AND CAUSES OF IMPORTANCE THEN
ARE THINGS I CAN'T REMEMBER

IN A WORLD THAT DIDN'T WORK
IT SEEMED THAT NOTHING FIT
OF ALL THE CANDLES THAT I BURNED
I SEARCH FOR ANY LIT

WHERE LOVE AND PASSION LED ME ON
NOW A WARM EMBRACE IS FINE
ONE SWEET KISS OR GENTLE HUG
ASSURES ME THAT SHE'S MINE

YET, I WON'T LET GO OF EVERYTHING
PERHAPS THERE IS A REASON WHY
FOR THERE IS BEAUTY IN THE EMBERS
JUST LIKE PEACE BEFORE I DIE

*Have you recently joined
Joseph's Journey?*

- - - - - - - - - - - - - - - - - - - -

*Joseph's Journey, Volume 1
Poetry of Hope, Help, Healing and Humor*

*Joseph's Journey, Volume 2
Psychological Concepts Expressed in Poetry*

*Joseph's Journey, Volume 3
A Look at the Flip Side of My Life*

*Joseph's Journey, Volume 4
A Look in My Rear View Mirror:
"Did I Just Waste a Precious Life –
That Kept Mine from Being Used"*

*Joseph's Journey, Volume 5
Parkinson's Up-Close:
Life Changing Events that Only
You and God Can Reconcile*

*Joseph's Journey, Volume 6
There's a Poem for That*

These books can be ordered by sending the name of the book(s) and your name and address with a check or money order for $7.95 + $2.95 shipping & handling (total = $10.90 per book) made payable to:

Everlasting Publishing
P.O. Box 965
Vancouver, WA 98666-0965
USA

Also available to purchase online:

everlastingpublishing.org

*9 7 8 0 9 8 2 4 8 4 4 8 7 *